Fresh Scent

Fresh Scent

Selected Haiku of Lee Gurga

edited by
Randy M. Brooks

Brooks Books
Decatur, Illinois

Publication Credits:

Grateful acknowledgment is made to the editors of the following publications in which some of these poems appeared in present or earlier versions: *An Anthology of Haiku by people of the United States and Canada, Iga/Uena Basho Festival Anthology, Canadian Writers' Journal, Chidori, Constanta Haiku Anthology, Daily Yomiuri* (Japan), *The Dallas Morning News, Frogpond, Geppo Haiku Journal, Haiku International* (Japan), *Haiku Zashi Zo, Heron Quarterly, Illinois Dental Journal, Mainichi Daily News* (Japan), *Mayfly, Midwest Haiku Anthology, Modern Haiku, Old Pond, Timepieces, Tundra, U.S. News & World Report, Windchimes, Woodnotes, World Haiku Contest Anthology.*

Some of the poems in this book were written with the support of a 1998 poetry fellowship from the Illinois Arts Council, a state agency. The author would like to express his sincere gratitude to the Council for its support.

Published by:
> Brooks Books
> 4634 Hale Drive
> Decatur, Illinois 62526

First edition available only in library clothbound binding.
International Standard Book Number: 0-913719-86-2

All rights, including electronic rights, reserved. No part of this book may be reproduced or transmitted by any means without the written permission of the author, editor, and publisher, except for brief passages quoted in reviews or scholarly articles.

Copyright © 1998 by Lee Gurga
Printed in the United States of America

dedicated to

my friends and neighbors
the people of Illinois

Acknowledgments

I would like to thank Jan Gurga, Robert Spiess, and Charles P. Trumbull for sharing their thoughts on individual poems, and Charles Rossiter for his encouragement.

—Lee Gurga
April 2, 1998

Editor's Introduction

With great pleasure Brooks Books inaugurates a new series of clothbound books featuring outstanding English language haiku poets with the publication of *Fresh Scent: Selected Haiku of Lee Gurga*. Each selected haiku book in this series will include the very best haiku by an author who has spent a significant portion of his or her life's work in this genre. It is our hope that readers will enjoy these top-quality haiku and develop an appreciation for each author's contributions to the growth of haiku in English.

Lee Gurga has been writing haiku for more than three decades, and in the last 15 years, he has achieved significant recognition for his contributions to English language haiku. As you can note from the credits to this book, he has received numerous awards for his haiku through international competitions and haiku organizations. In 1995, as Vice President of the Haiku Society of America, he helped organize the 1st International Joint Haiku Conference in Chicago, and in 1997, as President, he helped organize and lead a delegation of North American haiku writers and editors to the 2nd International Joint Haiku Conference in Tokyo. He was recently designated a 1998 Poetry Fellow by the Illinois Arts Council, an honor never before bestowed upon a writer in Illinois for his or her work in haiku.

In addition to his service to the international haiku community, Lee Gurga has achieved a distinctive place through the quality of his haiku. Applying a steadfast devotion to truthfulness in his writing, Lee Gurga works to perfect each haiku in order to create a meaningful experience for readers. He understands the importance of the inspiration of nature and the mystery of the seasons of life. He remains faithful to the spontaneous spirit of the original insights and perceptions of each haiku moment. Taken individually, each haiku can be savored for its own flavors, its special feelings, its unique emotion. Taken collectively, we trust that you will find in Gurga's haiku, a life of the poet, expressed with the integrity of lived experience in rural America.

One of the pleasures of editing and publishing a poet's selected haiku is the very process of selecting the haiku to be included in the book. In this case, the author began by gathering his best published and unpublished haiku to be considered as possible selections. Then we recruited the assistance of two haiku editors, Robert Spiess and Charles Trumbull, who graciously reviewed and rated each of these possible selections. Taking these evaluations into consideration, Lee and I then reduced the number of poems from about 350 to the current 135 haiku selected for this publication. We did not select haiku according to publication credits, nor even on the basis of awards that might have been won. We did not select haiku to show the difference from earlier work to later work. We did not attempt to select haiku in order to demonstrate the range of experimentation with form. Each haiku was selected for its own merit.

Haiku originated from the Japanese linked verse called *renga*. In this collection we have arranged the haiku by attempting to use the linking and shifting techniques developed over the centuries by renga poets. These techniques include linking by word, content, scent, reflection, scenic or narrative extension. Although this book is not linked verse, we hope that the use of linking techniques will enrich the reader's overall experience. This arrangement insures a freshness to each haiku, as well as a movement within the seasons of the author's perceptions.

The foremost pleasure of publishing this book is, of course, the haiku themselves which are the products of Lee Gurga's lifelong passion and work in the genre. Gurga's haiku maintain a balance between the insight of spontaneous experience and the musical polish of well-crafted poetry. The original moment happens as suddenly as a flash of lightning or the swish of a cow's tail, but the final haiku is crafted not merely to record that moment but to make it come alive again for us, the readers. We are grateful to Lee for his gifts to us, these haiku from rural America.

—*Randy M. Brooks, Editor*
Decatur, Illinois
April 6, 1998

Table of Contents

Editor's Introduction 7

Preface 13

Haiku 17

Appendix

About Haiku 117

Preface

To write haiku, that is more than a few, more than once in awhile, takes several angles of the mind. One must, for example, be a noticer, often of small things, quick things, temporary things or conditions of a moment—here and then gone. One must think of the significance of moments—of the first day of school, the duck swimming in the cattle pen, the Amishmen whispering in their beards.

One must have that slant of eye that wants to know what these things mean, but in their own terms, not by application of some abstraction. The idea flowers from the observation, which is what the poet supplies. Walking alone, one notices the "tattered goldenrod / covered with dust." One doesn't comment on the feelings of loneliness or mortality that the old weeds radiate, but we clearly feel them.

One must be interested in people, the curve of their backs, the way their hands look when idle, the quirky things they will occasionally do, the philosophic drunk finally running out of gas, the dentists at a conference all washing their hands, the man hitchhiking south in his wheelchair as winter approaches.

One must also be quick to perceive humor and perhaps have a wry turn of mind. One notices that the roommate returns from his date with his underwear on inside out. One sees one's old girlfriend now with her girlfriend. One sees, working away at the mountain cherry, branch by branch, the photographer, and one saves him to the end of the poem. We cannot help but laugh. It isn't a bird after all.

It helps as well to have a kindliness, a warm nature that reaches out mentally to the little boy in the ripening wheat alone and simply sees him there, for the moment the center of the universe under the hazy moon. He is one of the truly important things going on in the world, the soul of little-boyness. Waking on Christmas morning, holding someone's hand, captures family love and domesticity in that one image.

One has to be aware that the conditions of natural life around us reflect the moods of our lives. Such an attitude of mind perceives the likeness between the bike in the grass with one wheel slowly turning and the summer afternoon on which this is observed. Growth, youth, a bit of laziness all are present. Or the tick on the dog's ear slowly filling with blood encapsulates the sultry afternoon on which the poet observed this event.

The haiku poet learns to say by not saying, to see the universal by stating the individual, the small, the slight, the passing event. Such a poet trusts the agility and imagination of the reader, who will be able to expand from his stated perception to supply a small world whirling around it, giving it meaning from his hint of meaning, following the pointing of his finger to the horizon.

In general, there are two things going on in haiku: the bitter morning and moving the injured puppy into the sun. Or the stunning beauty of the little waterfall and the wondering of others why the viewers are not speaking. Gurga's poems all illustrate this property, as well as the others mentioned above.

This is a book of poems to be read and reread. The fourth or fifth reading will be more rewarding than the first, because the finer weave of the poems will be clearer then. It is a textbook example of good haiku poetry, reflecting the poet's longtime acquaintance with the form in its many manifestations, as well as his own finely tuned nature. For such a poet, everyday life is rich with perceptions and associations, and his warm and friendly personality infuse his perceptions with humanity and charm.

These poems are especially rich in a sense of domestic relations, love, family, pets, profession, surroundings. He is very much a Midwestern poet, an Illinois poet. Not only are its seasons, weather, and temperatures plentiful in the poems, but the hay bales, stubble, alfalfa, barns, distant train sounds, ponds, herons, hidden birds' nests, and typically Midwestern people are present. And the poet comments on them in the usual understated Illinois manner, slightly laconic, though without an Edgar Lee Masters' cynicism or a Carl Sandburg's slamming in of harsh impressions. We laugh with him. We purse our lips, or raise our eyebrows at his insights, and we, like him, say little, though we often chuckle.

Lee Gurga has been writing haiku for a long time, and has contributed significantly to the Haiku Society of America in various offices and conferences. I first met him many years ago when he was still a college student studying under Professor Shozo Sato who was introducing various aspects of Japanese culture to Midwestern audiences. Lee came with Professor Sato to Principia College, in Illinois, where I was teaching, and acted, as I recall, as a kabuki dancer. Clearly the impulse of Japanese poetry didn't fade from his thought when he went on to become a dentist, but has grown to be a significant part not only of his life but of the haiku life of the Midwest and of America.

This present book is the latest of his contributions. I found the poems a real pleasure to read for their deft touch, their depth, their knack of putting the finger of the mind on the heart of the situation and saying, "There, there it is." This is what haiku strives to do, and these poems do it very well.

—Paul O. Williams
Belmont, California
February 26, 1998

haiku

fresh scent—
   the labrador's muzzle
     deeper into snow

my dream
awakens me . . .
I wake you

summer sunrise . . .
through morning haze
a bobwhite calls again

head down to the grass,
the young colt's flaxen tail
swatting . . . swatting . . .

winter coming on—
a man hitchhiking south
in his wheelchair

rural interstate—
all the other cars
exit together

frosty morning—
a snail stretches out
into the sun

rotted stump—
brown pint bottle
still hidden inside

television light
flickers on my children's faces—
autumn sunset

wedding picture:
each face finds
a different camera

white-haired nun—
in German still
her childhood prayers

the smell of the iron
as I come down the stairs—
winter evening

first snow—
little boy laughing
in his sleep

Christmas blizzard—
everything white
except his cheeks

his room empty now . . .
in the distance, points of light
on the interstate

the sound of rain
moving through the wheatstubble;
a night of love

summer dawn—
the curve of your body
under the sheets

first feeding—
smelling her milk
the black cat

summer grasses—
a clutch of mottled eggs
slowly stirring

fresh mown hay—
half a prairie kingsnake
in afternoon sun

closing-out auction—
the farmer clenches the muscles
in his cheek

professional conference—
in the restroom all the dentists
washing their hands

grandma's funeral—
shaking hands with the cousins
I don't remember

street magician—
tourists appear
disappear

morning calm . . .
heavy with frost the leaves
continue to fall

horse slobber
frozen to my coveralls—
New Year's Eve

arc of a rubberband
back and forth across the room;
winter evening

parading the stallion—
all eyes on
his dangling member

sultry afternoon—
a tick on the dog's ear
filling with blood

fluttering madly—
   butterfly in the slipstream
    of a passing freight

four or five turkeys
roosting in a leafless tree—
winter evening

Christmas morning—
bird dog in the stubblefield
chasing sparrows

frozen ground—
with every step
the thorn

while you sleep
the gentle rocking
of the night train

20th anniversary—
doing sit-ups together
in perfect time

pine shade—
the wooden bench
worn smooth

opossum bones
wedged in an upper fork—
budding leaves

on the second day
I buy a deck of cards—
spring rain

postal chess—
he moves me
from his cell

summer afternoon—
the name of some town
spelled out in flowers

Amish waitress—
black dress stretching down
to her Reeboks

figure drawing class—
in the model's deepest shadow
a stark white string

moonrise . . .
sagging bales black
to the meadow's end

morning twilight . . .
horse asleep in the pasture
covered with frost

silent prayer—
the quiet humming
of the ceiling fan

cutting posts—
the sizzle of sleet
on the chainsaw housing

our tangled bodies
motionless in the bed;
coffee brewing

against the rumbling
of the thunderhead:
his toy gun

as the light fails,
still hammering
from the treehouse

storm windows
stacked against the house—
spring sunset

lawn furniture
without any cushions—
cherries leafing out

a bike in the grass
one wheel slowly turning—
summer afternoon

a little boy
alone in the ripening wheat—
hazy moon

hidden waterfall—
they come to see
why we're not speaking

exploring the cave . . .
my son's flashlight beam
disappears ahead

chopping out stumps—
the old boundary dispute
with every stroke

still water
reflects the sky . . .
I begin to forget

pushing in walnuts
with my heel—
autumn rain

blackberry picking—
the first breath of morning
in the cottonwood tops

abandoned still—
broken mason jars
sparkle in the moss

the sky black with stars—
coyote tracks up and down
the frozen creek

a duck swimming
in the cattle pen—
spring rain

blast of wind
flattens the roadside grass—
hitchhiker on her suitcase

last bale of hay—
we sit down on it
and watch the moon

summer harbor—
each boat pointing
to the storm

rows of corn
stretch to the horizon—
sun on the thunderhead

long walk alone—
a tattered goldenrod
covered with dust

from the tall weeds
the smell of something dead—
autumn afternoon

the liquid movement
of the raccoon's eyes:
filled with maggots

running with the car—
the black tip of the dog's tail
through knee-high corn

scenic overlook—
the whole Mississippi valley
hidden in mist

a spot of sunlight—
on a blade of grass the dragonfly
changes its grip

legs pawing
in the summer wind—monarch
in the wiper blade

midday sun—
butterflies flutter about
the peeing boy

the longest day—
a mother calls and calls
into the night

school bus gone;
the old cedar
in & out of fog

                        "There's the comet . . ."
                        the little boy watches
                        his father's breath

winter prairie—
a diesel locomotive
throttles down in the night

Christmas morning—
we wake up holding
each other's hand

one nipple
against the white cotton—
dark halo of milk

summer sunset—
the baby finds his shadow
on the kitchen wall

winter sun begins
to warm the steering wheel—
prison visit day

Visitor's Room—
everything bolted down
except my brother

another Christmas . . .
my parents visit
the son in prison

spit on the whetstone—
the little boy tests an edge
on the birthday knife

call after call.
finally, my six year-old's
"Lee Gurga!"

night sounds—
I put another blanket
on the sleeping boy

tourist motel—
the pattern of the bedspread
on your cheek

mountain cherry—
from branch to branch
the photographer

snowbound—
firelight on the face
of the sleeping boy

hair stubble
on the deodorant stick:
the heat

birthday shopping—
into the dress she loves
her daughter's hips

home from a date—
my roommate's underwear
now inside out

the philosophic drunk
finally runs out of gas . . .
cicadas

dry riverbed—
great blue heron in a puddle
staring back at me

the end of my lane—
I open the sagging gate
to autumn sunset

after my walk:
a perfect spiderweb
stuck to my glasses

everyone asleep
except the one sleeping alone—
distant train whistles

now that you've left,
your side of the bed covered
with open books

farm dog calling
calling to her echo
deep in the forest

spring horse auction—
a cluster of Amishmen whispering
through their beards

sweat steaming
from a team of geldings;
endless stars

snow-packed roads—
the wind blows through
a stripped Camaro

cold drizzle—
a puff of diesel smoke
rises from the freight

frozen branches
measure the emptiness—
winter sunset

autumn rain—
old man's furniture
in the pickup

Thanksgiving Day—
the whole family silent
watching a football game

afternoon sun—
squirrel on a slab of snow
sliding down the roof

country stop sign—
the pink glow of sunset
through .22 holes

boy shooting baskets—
deep snow piled
all around him

I read
she reads
winter evening

Transfiguration—
candle flames bend and rise
with the church's breath

Sunday afternoon—
asking his father the name
of every flower

the dog runs ahead—
old roadbed through the forest
deep with leaves

dozing off . . .
one hand on your skin
and on your silk

darkness before dawn—
the way your legs sleep
not closed   not open

morning mist . . .
the soft brown eye
of the suckling calf

candlelight dinner—
his finger slowly circles
the rim of his glass

his side of it.
her side of it.
winter silence

Christmas pageant—
the one who had to get married
plays Mary

                              the end
                              of moving day;
                              dogs barking

bitter morning—
I move the injured puppy
into the sun

trying the old pump a mouse pours out

restored prairie . . .
where the grasses end
the prison's outer fence

fishermen's cars
parked along the roadside—
cold rain at sunset

fresh-baled hay—
cutting the twine
to let the snake go

moon gazing . . .
the dog keeps trying
to lead us away

spring rain—
stepping over barbed wire
into the woods

weekend with their dad—
the boys go deeper
into the mountain

two boys   the last pile of dirty snow

graduation day—
my son & I side by side
knotting our ties

class reunion—
with my old girlfriend
her girlfriend

the ticking of sleet
on the bedroom window;
your hand
gathers
me

    from house
       to barn:
          the milky way

Appendix

About Haiku

Introduction

Haiku occupies a unique position in American culture. A few childhood favorites aside, the average person today would rather have a tooth pulled than read a contemporary poem. But, while Americans in general have little interest in contemporary poetry, most have at least heard of haiku and often have a surprising affection for it. They will usually know that it is a somewhat exotic short poem, and that it has something to do with nature. Familiarity with haiku is so widespread, it was recently suggested that when Phil Jackson, the contemplative coach of the Chicago Bulls basketball team was ready to retire, he would withdraw to the mountains of Montana and compose haiku! This mention of haiku in *Sports Illustrated* assumes a familiarity with haiku even among the sports audience, generally not known for its devotion to literature. It also suggests that haiku is not merely a "form" of poetry, but that the haiku tradition also contains some elements of philosophy.

What is haiku?

For most people, haiku is a form of poetry, a three line poem made up of 17 syllables in a 5-7-5 pattern. Haiku can be this, but this form does not define all of what haiku is. Those of you who may have been counting syllables as you were reading this book already know that not many of the poems in it are 17 syllables. I will try to explain what makes these poems, and other poems like them, haiku.

Haiku, as almost everyone knows, is a short poem that originated in Japan. Japanese haiku began as the opening verse of a long linked poem. These haiku had several defining characteristics including their brevity and a seasonal reference. Poets writing haiku in English over the past 40 years have distilled several characteristics out of these Japanese haiku which they consider to be the essence of haiku. An understanding of these characteristics allows poets today to write a special kind of

117

haiku, one that uses "images that reflect intuitions" to present the essence of a single moment of time.

These essential haiku characteristics include brevity, a seasonal or nature reference, the "haiku moment," juxtaposition, and what is referred to as "haiku mind."

Originally haiku was not an isolated form of Japanese poetry, but it was part of a larger tradition called *haikai* which included the linked verse from which haiku developed as well as another short poetic form called senryu. Senryu is similar to haiku in form, but different in that it relies less on imagistic presentation of natural scenes and more on the poet's wit. I would like to say a little about each of these elements of the haiku tradition.

Season

The seasonal reference was originally included in haiku to evoke the time of the year in which the poem was composed. But some poets, beginning with the great Japanese haiku master Bashō, realized that the seasonal reference contained within it the seeds of something much more powerful. By connecting the experience of a single moment to the universal forces of change and renewal, the seasonal reference has developed into haiku's most powerful tool to engage the reader: it allows the poet to invoke the whole of the natural world with a single image.

In spite of the fact that most people today have chosen to spend their lives going from one man-made environment to another, many people still have a longing for some contact with nature. While it may be more difficult for people who live in an urban environment to be conscious of the natural world, nature pervades every aspect of our lives whether we are aware of it or not. Haiku allow us to explore and enrich our relationship with nature whether it is through the peace of mind one develops hiking in the mountains or the annoyance of having been caught trying to hail a cab in the rain without an umbrella. Contemporary haiku try to maintain the seasonal reference while producing a poem that is contemporary in both tone and subject

Haiku Moment

Haiku tries to record a singular experience, the haiku moment. When people first attempt to write haiku, they often write poems based on the ironic situations they encounter, since those are the ones most likely to command their attention. But these ironic situations are not the source of true haiku.

What is a haiku moment? Ralph Waldo Emerson wrote in his Journals, "There is a difference between one and another hour of life in their authority and subsequent effect. Our faith comes in moments; our vice is habitual. Yet there is a depth in those brief moments which constrains us to ascribe more reality to them than to all other experiences." James Joyce called these moments "epiphanies." Nobel prize-winning poet Czeslaw Milosz says of epiphanies, "Epiphany is an unveiling of reality. What in Greek was called *epiphaneia* meant the appearance, the arrival, of a divinity among mortals or its recognition under a familiar shape of man or woman. Epiphany thus interrupts the everyday flow of time and enters as one privileged moment when we intuitively grasp a deeper, more essential reality hidden in things or persons." These moments are the genuine haiku moments.

Juxtaposition

Haiku present images to convey emotions. The primary technique used to convey these emotions is the juxtaposition or "internal comparison" of two or more images. The interaction between these two images creates a space in which the reader's emotions can grow. Of course, the relationship between the two images cannot be too close and obvious, or the poem will have no real interest; on the other hand, if the relationship is too distant, the association of the images will appear forced and arbitrary to the reader.

There are several ways in which the two images can interact successfully. In a more traditional haiku, where the second image reinforces the first in mood or tone, we often get a poem that is rather subdued, like this one:

    pine shade—
    the wooden bench
    worn smooth

However, if the second interacts with the first in a way that is unexpected, the poem can carry us off in a startling new trajectory like that produced in a cloud chamber by the collision of high-energy particles. This kind of haiku creates a certain expectation with the first image, then carries us off to an entirely unexpected place with the second:

> dancing to my tune
> cricket
> in the urinal

This juxtaposition of images is accomplished by a technique called "cutting," which divides the poem into two parts. This can be accomplished in any of several ways in English, using grammar, punctuation, spacing or line breaks. This cutting allows for the juxtaposition of images or internal comparison that characterize most fine haiku. Cutting or juxtaposition is considered by many to be the primary technique of haiku.

Haiku Mind

A haiku is the record of an event. But it is not simply a journalistic report. Objective presentation is not enough: the event must be combined with the poet's mind to produce what Basho called *yojo*, or "surplus meaning." If the event we record is memorable in itself, the contribution of the poet's mind is relatively small. If the event itself has little overt significance, the contribution of the poet's mind becomes a greater factor in producing a poem that communicates significance to the reader.

I have found that the poems I appreciate most are those that combine seemingly insignificant events with the poet's mind in such a way that the hidden significance of these events is unfolded for the reader. How does one do this? Contemporary haiku master Yatsuka Ishihara says that real truth exists only in the "landscape of our hearts." Therefore, we will be able to capture the true significance of things if we look at the world with our hearts rather than with our minds.

Senryu

Fine short poems can result from the combination of wit with precise observation. These poems, especially when they focus on the humor of human relations, are called *senryu*. Senryu is similar to haiku in origin (in that both originated in linked poetry) and it is similar to haiku in form. But haiku and senryu differ dramatically both in content and in tone. Senryu emphasize human affairs rather than the relationship between people and nature. (While nature can be present in senryu, it is secondary or incidental to the human element.) Senryu often use satire to bring to our attention examples of the hypocrisy of human behavior or examples of what can be called "cosmic humor." While the best haiku will reverberate or carry the reader on past the end of the poem, the best senryu have a "snap" or "kick" at the end. This is often an easy way to tell haiku from senryu. Most of the poems in this collection are haiku, but some that have a surprise saved up for the reader in the third line, like:

>   class reunion—
>   with my old girlfriend
>   her girlfriend

are more appropriately considered senryu.

Haiku Spirit

Since everyday experience is the material of haiku, everyone is potentially a haiku poet. This makes haiku ideal for teaching in schools and prisons, nursing homes and bars. Because haiku record single moments of perception in short poems, they are an ideal form of expression for our "instant" society, in which people's attention span is tuned to shorter and more fragmented inputs. For some people, haiku is part of a spiritual path. For others it is a form of recreation. It can be a tool for sharpening one's powers of observation, perception, and expression. That haiku is large enough to contain all of these says something of the unique nature of haiku and is perhaps a key to understanding why some of us are carried away by haiku.

>   fluttering madly—
>   butterfly in the slipstream
>   of a passing freight

>   —*Lee Gurga*
>   *March 30, 1998*

About the Author

Lee Gurga was born and raised in Chicago, but has spent most of his adult life as a dentist with a practice in the small Midwestern town of Lincoln, Illinois. He currently lives in the country with wife Jan, sons Ben, A.J., and Alex, dog Fay and five haflinger horses. In addition to his studies to become a dentist, Dr. Gurga studied mathematics, Asian studies, and dance at the University of Illinois in Champaign-Urbana, Illinois. As part of his Asian studies program, he had the unique opportunity to study kabuki dance and tea ceremony under the direction of Shozo Sato.

Gurga first became interested in haiku in 1966, having found a copy of R.H. Blyth's translations of Japanese haiku on the shelf of a Chicago bookshop. Although he had been writing haiku on and off over the years, he did not start publishing until 1987.

He was soon receiving awards for his haiku, and High/Coo Press published his first collection, *a mouse pours out*, in 1988. In 1992 he was co-editor of *Midwest Haiku Anthology* (with Randy Brooks), also published by High/Coo Press. This book received second place in the Haiku Society of America Merit Book Awards for 1992. Gurga has also received first place in several competitions including the 1996 Haiku Summit Contest, the 1996 Canadian Writers' Journal Haiku Contest, the 1996 Kusamakura International Haiku Contest, and the 1990 Mainichi Daily News Haiku in English Contest. He received the 1995 Ito-en New Haiku Contest Jury's Choice Award which resulted in a brief story in the *U.S. News & World Report* including a photo of his haiku printed on a can of Ito-en tea. In 1998 he was honored with an Illinois Arts Council Poetry Fellowship for his work in haiku.

In 1988 he became active with the Haiku Society of America and help organize several 20th Anniversary gatherings in the Midwest. He served as Vice President of the Haiku Society of America in 1991 and again in 1995-96, and served as President in 1997. As a leader of HSA he was instrumental in organizing the HSA/Haiku International Association Joint Conference in Chicago in 1995, and in 1997 he led a delegation of prominent English language haiku poets and editors to the second Joint Conference in Tokyo. He is currently associate editor of *Modern Haiku*, the longest-running journal of haiku and haiku studies in English.

In addition to *a mouse pours out*, (High/Coo Press, 1988), the following collections of his haiku have been published: *In & Out of Fog* (Press Here, 1997), *Nine Haiku* (Swamp Press, 1997), *dogs barking* (Lidia Press, 1996), and *The Measure of Emptiness* (Press Here, 1991).

Award Credits

"fresh scent" .... (p. 19)
1st place 1996 Haiku Summit Haiku Contest (Intl. Division)

"television light" .... (p. 25)
honorable mention 1997 HEA Haiku Contest

"first snow" .... (p. 28)
honorable mention
1997 Canadian Writers' Journal Haiku Contest

"street magician" .... (p. 35)
honorable mention 1989 World Haiku Contest

"horse slobber" .... (p. 36)
honorable mention 1996 Haiku Splash haiku contest

"fluttering madly" .... (p. 39)
2nd place 1996 British Haiku Society Haiku contest

"four or five turkeys" .... (p. 40)
Jury's Choice Award 1995 Ito-en New Haiku Contest

"frozen ground" .... (p. 41)
honorable mention 1988 Japan Airlines Haiku Contest

"figure drawing class" .... (p. 47)
honorable mention 1989 Henderson Haiku Contest

"morning twilight" .... (p. 49)
3rd place 1996 Haiku Poets of Northern California Contest

"our tangled bodies" .... (p. 51)
honorable mention 1996 Haiku Splash Haiku Contest

"rows of corn" .... (p. 65)
grand prize 1996 Kusamakura International Haiku Contest

Award Credits (continued)

"running with the car" .... (p. 68)
high commendation Timepieces 1997 Haiku Contest

"summer sunset" .... (p. 75)
1st place 1990 *Mainichi Daily News* Haiku Contest

"winter sun begins" .... (p. 76)
honorable mention 1996 HEA Haiku Contest

"cold drizzle" .... (p. 90)
honorable mention 1996 *Mainichi Daily News* Haiku Contest

"Sunday afternoon" .... (p. 96)
3rd place 1997 Hawaii Educational Association Haiku Contest

"morning mist" .... (p. 99)
1st place 1996 Canadian Writers' Jounal Haiku Contest

"his side of it." .... (p. 101)
honorable mention
Haiku Poets of Northern California Senryu Contest

"the ticking of sleet" .... (p. 112)
honorable mention 1996 Haiku Splash Haiku Contest

Colophon

Book design and layout by Randy M. Brooks with the vigilant collaboration of Lee Gurga.

Printed in a limited first edition on acid-free paper and bound in Kivar cornmeal "Corinth" cloth by BookCrafters of Chelsea, Michigan.

The dust jacket was designed by Mike Thomas, a graphic design student at Millikin University, as a competitive assignment in a Commercial Art course taught by Professor Ed Walker.